Original title:
The Grapefruit's Secret

Copyright © 2025 Creative Arts Management OÜ
All rights reserved.

Author: Seraphina Caldwell
ISBN HARDBACK: 978-1-80586-382-3
ISBN PAPERBACK: 978-1-80586-854-5

Shadows of Citrus Glow

In the grove, a tale so bright,
Lemons gossip, oranges in sight.
A fruit with a grin, a rind with flair,
Hiding juicy laughs, beyond compare.

A citrus ball in a funny pose,
Dancing with joy, striking a pose.
Its zest brings splashes, a burst of cheer,
Tickling taste buds, far and near.

Unveiling the Zesty Heart

Peeling layers, a whiff of jest,
This playful fruit, the life of the fest.
With every slice, surprise takes flight,
Sour meets sweet in a zany bite.

Citrus chuckles in a sunlit tangle,
Winking at blooms, a curious mangle.
Juice that squirts with laughter's gleam,
Sparking joy like a wild dream.

Sweet Deceit of the Orchard

In the orchard where mischief grows,
A twist in the tale, nobody knows.
Rind so bright, with secrets sly,
A pucker of wit beneath the sky.

A slice reveals a giggling treat,
Juicy laughter, oh so sweet!
Nature's trickster with citrus charm,
Leaves us grinning, safe from harm.

Secrets of the Juicy Core

Beneath the skin, a secret plot,
Citrus giggles, oh, what a lot!
Each juicy wedge a punchline waits,
A fruit-shaped joke on our plates.

Peel back laughter, relishing glee,
This zesty tale, come join in free!
With every bite, let chuckles soar,
A laughter-fest we all adore.

Citrus Whispers

In the orchard where fruits like to chat,
A lemon said, 'Hey, I'm smarter than that!'
The orange rolled in with a laugh so grand,
'I've got zest, my friend, you just don't understand!'

The limes chimed in with a cheeky grin,
'We make drinks that let the good times begin!'
While grapefruits giggled in all of their glee,
'It's a zestful world, won't you come share with me?'

Hidden within Rind

Peeling back layers to find what's inside,
A treasure of flavors where secrets abide.
The tangy sweet bites all delightfully dance,
While citrus friends giggle, giving taste buds a chance.

Under the sunlight, the antics unfold,
As fruits toss their peels and the stories are told.
A grapefruit jokes, 'You'll never know why,
I hide all my jokes 'neath this zesty blue sky!'

The Eternal Juice

A fountain of fun with a splash of surprise,
The juice just laughs as it tries to disguise.
'You thought you could bottle me, oh, what a game!
I spill out my secrets with every new name!'

The tropics conspire in a fruity parade,
While juice-drunk enthusiasts dance unafraid.
So grab all your friends and just let out a cheer,
For juice flows eternal, it's perfectly clear!

Secrets Beneath the Zest

Under the skin, where the flavors reside,
A tangle of stories that fruits cannot hide.
The grapefruit giggles, a chuckle so sly,
'If you squeeze me too hard, I might just say bye!'

The peels have their whispers, a citrusy tease,
As they play 'hide and seek' with the warm summer breeze.
So come take a bite and savor each jest,
For life's more amusing beneath all the zest!

Orange Glow in Twilight

Beneath the sky of candy hue,
A citrus fruit did bid adieu.
It glowed like laughter, bright and bold,
With zestful tales just waiting to be told.

A squirrel passed by, with twitching nose,
He pondered where the juice fish flows.
Like Cupid's arrow, it struck with glee,
This fruity orb holds all the spree!

Round and plump, with vibrant cheer,
This sunny joy, we hold so dear.
Yet with each bite, a twist of fate,
A sour shock makes friends debate!

"Oh, go ahead, my tangy friend!"
The laughter waves, it has no end.
An orange winks, it hides the glee,
The twilight dances—you wait and see!

A Tangy Revelation

In the fridge, a bright delight,
A mystery wrapped in hues so tight.
When peeled, it giggles, plays a song,
A tangle of tastes that can't be wrong.

What lies beneath this skin so bright?
Puckering kisses, oh what a bite!
It teases tongues with playful zest,
A punchline hidden within its jest.

Friends assemble for this grand reveal,
Each slice, a burst—a juicy meal.
"Is it sweet? Is it sour?" they cheer,
The laughter erupts; it's crystal clear!

Citrus laughter fills the air,
With every wedge, we shed our care.
A tangy smile, a fruity cheer,
This round affair brings friends so near!

The Forbidden Slice

Behind the curtain, thrived a fruit,
With forbidden charm and stealthy loot.
A slice so bright, it called my name,
In hushed tones, it played its game.

The table groaned with wonders rare,
But this bold orb hid in its lair.
"Have a taste!" it serenely beckoned,
While sneaky thoughts, around me, reckoned.

Whispers of sweetness danced like spies,
"Just one taste, you won't despise!"
With guile and glee, I took a chance,
This fruity rogue led me in a dance!

But oh, the twist! It stung, it stunned,
Sweet and sour—a mind unspun.
We giggled wild, my fate embraced,
A forbidden slice, I gladly faced!

Elixir of the Sun

In the morn, I found the light,
A potion bright, a sunny sight.
Sippin' joy from citrus cups,
A zesty cheer, it bubbles up!

With each woozy sip, I dance,
A tangy twirl, a dizzy chance.
It whispers tales of lazy days,
Where sunshine plays and laughter stays.

Oh, elixir, sweet and bright,
You chase the shadows with delight.
In orange rivers, we float and swirl,
With fruity secrets that twist and twirl!

So raise your cup, let friendship bloom,
With every sip, we banish gloom.
This sunny gift, we won't refuse,
An orange toast that we all choose!

Unveiling the Orange Veil

Underneath a peely mask,
Lies a treasure, oh so bright.
With each slice, it gives a laugh,
A tangy burst, a pure delight.

Seeds like confetti scatter wide,
A party inside, oh what a tease!
Juicy giggles, can't decide,
To munch or sip, it's sure to please.

The Zest of Revelation

Peeling layers, what a show,
A squirt of juice, it's pure delight.
With every bite, the laughter flows,
Zesty vibes dance in the light.

Mysterious orb with a sunlit face,
Poking the pulp, mischievous fun.
Make a mess, embrace the grace,
In this circus, we are all one.

Citrus Whispers

In the bowl, a bold charade,
Wobbling orbs with a citrus grin.
Squeezed too hard, a lemon shade,
Oops! A splash, let fun begin.

Whispers tingle from the zest,
This fruit's a joker in disguise.
Bubbling giggles are the best,
Spilling secrets, sunshine flies.

Beneath the Zest

Beneath the rind, a tale unfolds,
Of citrus pranks and fruity cheer.
Jokes and jests, in sweetness told,
Slice it open, laughter's near.

Pithy punchlines, a comic twist,
Peeling laughter, can't resist.
A juicy world where smiles persist,
Fruity fun we can't dismiss.

Echoes of Citrus Dreams

In the groves where laughter grows,
Fruits wear smiles, nobody knows.
A twist, a turn, a citrus spin,
Secrets wrapped in rind and grin.

With every bite, a joke unfolds,
Tales of tanginess, bold and told.
Lemon laughter, orange cheer,
In this land, fun is near.

Peeling layers, what do we find?
Thoughts of zest, and silly mind.
Wedges of wonder, ripe and free,
Fruity giggles, come and see!

So join the feast, the fruity flair,
Let's dance with flavor, everywhere.
In every sip, a punchline waits,
Echoes of dreams on citrus plates.

The Tang of Untold Stories

Beneath the skin of bright delight,
Lemon jokes and orange light.
Puns get zesty, sour and sweet,
Where citrus fun and laughter meet.

The tales they tell of fruit so round,
Of juicy secrets, lost and found.
A slice of pure, a giggle burst,
Refreshing quips, our flavor thirst.

In gardens green, they dance and play,
Hiding laughter in the spray.
With every roll and every sway,
They tickle tongues in a fruity way.

So crack a peel, and sip the joy,
Citrus whispers, oh what a ploy!
With every tang, a chuckle ripe,
Untold stories take the type.

Enigmatic Citrus Spirits

In a grove with nuts in sight,
Citrus shadows dance at night.
Limes conspiring, oranges laugh,
Pineapple plotting their own path.

With pithy tales, they run and roll,
Juggling flavors, playing a role.
A tangerine on a wild spree,
Mixing up secrets, oh my glee!

Mysterious fruits in masks of zest,
Whispering jokes, they know the best.
In every sip, a spirit sings,
Of funky fruits and joyful things.

So raise your glass and toast with cheer,
To enigmatic fun that's ever near.
For in the spirit of citrus, bright,
Lies the laughter that ignites the night.

Citrus Echoes of Joy

In the orchard, laughter sprays,
Citrus giggles fill the bays.
Oranges chuckle, lemons tease,
Rind-wrapped joy, a playful breeze.

With every twist, a joke emerges,
Sour secrets, whimsy surges.
Peel back layers, find the fun,
In this feast, we are all one.

Splashes of color, bright and bold,
In every fruit, the stories told.
A splash of zest, a hint of fun,
In citrus echoes, joy's begun.

So gather round, the fruits we share,
With citrus kindness, love in the air.
Raise your cup, and take a sip,
To citrus joy and comedy's grip.

The Sweetness Within

In a citrus world so bright,
A fruit hides with all its might.
Peel it back, what a surprise,
A sweet burst right before your eyes.

Juicy gems with zestful glee,
In every section, nature's spree.
Laugh as you squint, juice goes astray,
A tangy fight, oh what a play!

Sour faces turn to bliss,
One little bite, you can't miss.
Like a prankster in the sun,
It tricks you, then it's all in fun!

Wrap it up with zestful cheer,
A fruity giggle, lend an ear.
With every bite, you soon will find,
A sweetness that will leave you blind!

Tangy Tales of Yore

Once upon a citrus dream,
A tale began with a bright gleam.
Covered in a bumpy coat,
It whispered secrets, so remote!

With every twist, it would confide,
A twangy story deep inside.
Lemon's cousin, dressed so proud,
Shared its wit among the crowd.

Rind so thick, you'd never guess,
Funny jokes in tart finesse.
Slice it open, giggles flow,
It's more than just a fruity show!

Every bite, a laugh, a treat,
Citrus tales, oh what a feat!
So dive right in, don't be late,
Discover fun upon your plate!

Revelations in Citrus Aroma

In the garden where laughs bloom,
A fragrant orb dispels the gloom.
Peeling layers, a whiff so sly,
A burst of giggles, oh my, oh my!

Sour notes dance in the air,
Mischief lurking everywhere.
Each slice calls you to come near,
Join the fun, let's spread some cheer!

Zesty whispers float around,
A funny fruit, where joy is found.
With every squeeze, a chuckle's made,
Citrus secrets never fade.

So take a bite, let laughter brew,
In every morsel, joy rings true.
Behind the peel, a laughing spree,
Unravel fun, just you and me!

Beneath the Bright Peel

Beneath the skin, a tale unfolds,
Of sweetness wrapped in citric molds.
Its cheerful hue, a wink and jest,
With every fruit, it's bound to test.

Pop the top, what do you see?
A squirt of laughter, wild and free.
Juice goes flying, what a sight,
A citrus comedy, so delight!

In the bowl, they play around,
Making faces, quite profound.
Each segment giggles, sings a song,
With zestful rhythms, can't go wrong!

So savor bites, and let it show,
That fruit can bring a funny flow.
Here's to peels that hide away,
The joy that greets you every day!

Palate of Secrets

In the fruit bowl, bright and bold,
A tale of zest, waiting to unfold.
With a grin so wide, like a playful tease,
It whispers truths, like a teasing breeze.

Each slice a promise, sweet yet strange,
Fragrant laughter, in every range.
With every bite, the secrets pour,
Juicy surprises, who could ask for more?

Dance of flavors, a citrus show,
Pucker up, let the fun flow!
With a wink and a twist, it leads the way,
To a world where humor comes out to play.

The Color of Hidden Truths

Orange peels guard the giggles inside,
In every segment, the jokes do abide.
Bright colors hide the laughs so true,
Under the surface, they're ready for you.

Sour and sweet, a paradox bold,
These vibrant spheres, with tales to be told.
A splash of sunshine, a twist of the knife,
Making mundane days feel awfully rife.

Like a clown in a fruit hat, here to delight,
Every juicy mouthful makes the world light.
Closer we gather, with giggles that sprout,
This fruit's not just tasty, but it's a riot, no doubt!

Sweet Citrus Reverie

In dreams of yellow, I don't mind the weight,
Of drippy citrus tides that taste so great.
Each spoonful's laughter, tangy delight,
Dancing on tongues, oh what a sight!

Beneath the sun, we laugh and we twirl,
Juicy confessions in every swirl.
Sassy and zesty, with giggles galore,
This merry fruit is never a bore.

Whispers and bubbles, they playfully tease,
Offering sweetness, aiming to please.
In this fruity frolic, the fun never ends,
A citrusy journey with all of our friends.

The Essence of Joy

Lemons may frown, but I'm here to cheer,
With a citrus delight that steers the sphere.
In every round orb, joy hides within,
Bursting with humor, oh let's begin!

Slicing through smiles, we savor the fun,
Every segment's a blast, oh what a run!
Witty and funny, a tart little grin,
Summoning laughter from deep within.

With a spritz of zest, we twist and we shout,
In a fruit medley, we dance about.
Whirling with joy, we savor each bite,
In this zany escapade, everything feels right!

The Pulse of Citrus

In the orchard where they dance,
Round and round, they take a chance.
With a twist and a playful pout,
They whisper tales, yet never shout.

Sunshine bursts from juicy sheen,
Each slice, a giggle, bright and keen.
Beneath their skin, a story hides,
Of tart romance where sweetness bides.

They bounce and roll on kitchen floor,
With zesty laughs, they beg for more.
A citrus chorus sings with glee,
They know the joy of being free.

In every bite, a quirky jest,
A taste that's lively, never rest.
So pick a fruit that knows to play,
And let its humor brighten your day.

Secrets Bursting in Flesh

Underneath that dimpled skin,
A comedy awaits within.
With each delicious, orange grin,
It's time to feast, let the fun begin.

They hold confessions, juicy tales,
Of summer days and wind-swept gales.
A wink of tartness, sweet reveal,
These secret spheres know how to feel.

Caught in a salad, playing tricks,
Or splashed in drinks for citrus kicks.
Their laughter travels through your snack,
Unlock the joy, there's no comeback.

With every bite, the giggles whirl,
These fruity jesters start to twirl.
So tuck them in your tote today,
Let fruity secrets lead the way!

Enigma of the Orchard

In a grove where odd things grow,
Citrus custards line the row.
With riddles sharp, they light the way,
Mysteries wrapped in zesty play.

A peel can hide a chuckle tight,
Jokes awaiting in every bite.
They twist and turn, will you take heed?
The orchard's laughter plants a seed.

Mysterious, they tempt the taste,
A brisk delight with zest to waste.
Discover flavors, giggle and munch,
In every slice, a citrus punch.

So gather round, come one, come all,
For fruity banter that won't fall.
The enigma lingers in the air,
Unlock the fun, if you dare!

A Peel of Mystery

Beneath the skin, the laughter hides,
With every slice, the joy abides.
A peel that's bright, a tale that spins,
Where whimsy lives and fun begins.

Citrus capers, bursting free,
A zest-filled dance of glee and spree.
They bat their eyes and wave hello,
With sly confessions in their glow.

Let's stir the bowl, a playful mess,
Smooth the surface, but don't suppress.
These fruits hold mysteries in their core,
Unraveling laughs, always more in store.

So peel away, embrace the fun,
In every nibble, there's a pun.
Let citrus secrets light your way,
And join the joy, this merry play!

In the Realm of Citrus Whimsy

In a grove where fruits play games,
A wobbly lemon shouts out names.
The orange giggles, full of zest,
While limes perform a citrus jest.

They bounce and roll, the fun begins,
As grapefruits plot their silly skins.
A tango here, a cha-cha there,
All fruits unite in fruity flair.

But deep inside the grapefruit's heart,
Lies a riddle, a puzzling art.
With whispers sweet, it teases so,
"Guess my flavor, and you shall know!"

So join the dance, don't miss the chance,
To make a fruit bowl take a stance.
With laughter loud and jumps galore,
In citrus land, you'll crave for more!

Savoring Unspoken Citrus

In a market bustling, so alive,
Citrus lovers take a dive.
With tangy tales of orange cheer,
And whispers shared that only they hear.

Lemons gossip, oh so bright,
While grapefruits hide, just out of sight.
"Am I sweet? Am I sour?"
"What's my fate? Will I be devoured?"

A lime rolls over, eyes a-dream,
"Is there more to life than just a squeeze?"
While tangerines burst out with zest,
In this fruit fest, they're all the best!

So let's peel back the layers thick,
And savor each citrusy trick.
For in each bite, a giggle flows,
Unspoken secrets, everyone knows!

Beyond the Peel's Guarded Secrets

A grapefruit lounged in a sunlit glade,
With a sly grin, it planned its parade.
"I'll trick the world with my lively hue,
While hiding truths like a playful clue!"

The oranges chuckled, the lemons rolled,
"Let's see what secrets your peel can hold!"
As they launched into a citrus race,
The grapefruit wobbled, wearing a face.

"Am I juicy? Am I bland?"
"Take a taste, it's a mystery grand!"
Their laughter echoed through the trees,
As they dived in pools of citrus breeze.

So peel away the guarded lies,
And find the joy that citrus applies.
With each bright bite, let humor flow,
Beyond the skin, the fun will grow!

The Sublime Bittersweet

In a world of pith and zest,
A citrus hero brings its best.
With a sour grin, it winks at me,
A fruity jest, oh can't you see?

Peeling layers, oh what a sight,
Bitter laughs by morning light.
An orb of cheer with taste profound,
In every bite, pure joy is found.

Juicy giggles drip from my face,
A giddy dance, oh what a place!
Sipping juice with glee and grace,
I'm in a citrusy embrace.

So next time you take a slice,
Do beware, it may entice.
With bittersweet and laughter shared,
In fruit-filled joys, we're always paired.

Unsung Citrus Poetics

In the orchard, whispers grow,
Citrus tales no one can know.
Lemons laugh at their own plight,
While oranges take flight of night.

The tangy truth shall always spill,
A fruit like this can surely thrill.
With each drop, a punchline swift,
Squeezing hearts through every lift.

Mundane moments turn to cheer,
Spitting seeds will draw you near.
In every round and juicy core,
Lies a giggle, and maybe more.

So raise a glass to zest and tease,
Ferocious fruit that aims to please.
With nature's humor on the vine,
We toast the sweetness of our time.

A Slice of Forgotten Dreams

Once a dream, now a fruit so bold,
A slice of sun with tales untold.
It beckons with a vibrant hue,
Offering fragrant giggles too.

Cracking smiles with every bite,
Citrus sparks, oh what a sight!
Lost dreams swirl upon my tongue,
In juiced-up fun, we're always young.

Memories swirl like citrus zest,
Laughter's gift, a fruity fest.
Each grin a circle, round and true,
Happiness — the secret brew.

So let's indulge, let worries fade,
In fruity joy, we're unafraid.
A slice of cheer, let's all unite,
In the juicy dance of pure delight.

Mellow Hues of Deception

Beneath the skin, a riddle hides,
Where sweet meets sour, laughter abides.
It winks and nods, a playful tease,
This fruit of jest brings us to ease.

A mellow hue, with a chuckle bold,
Its citrus soul, a tale retold.
Biting in, you think it sweet,
But pucker up! Oh, what a treat!

With every drop, a giggle flows,
Deceptive joy in every pose.
Round and bright, it waltzes in,
Drawing laughter from within.

So here's to hues of amusing fate,
With fruits that dance, oh isn't it great?
Let's celebrate the funny spree,
In citrus fun, we just can't flee.

Hidden in the Rind

Underneath a sunny skin,
A twisty truth begins within.
Citrus giggles, bursting bright,
Jokes of zest, a playful bite.

Surprises lurk in every bite,
Mischief hidden, pure delight.
Sour whispers, sweetened cheer,
Let's peel away our doubts and fear.

Juicy chunks, a laughing spree,
Taste the truth, come dance with me!
Each segment holds a funny tale,
Squeeze the joy, let laughter sail.

Chasing flavors, having fun,
In this dance, we're all just one.
So come and share this fruity game,
Life's a punchline, enjoy the fame.

Sweet Pulp Confessions

In the midst of juicy seams,
Secrets bubble up like dreams.
Squirting juice and giggles flow,
Pulp confessions steal the show.

Each sticky drop, a whispered jest,
Hints of humor, oh so zest!
Crowned in wedges, sweet and round,
Taste of laughter, life unbound.

Peel my layers, find the fun,
Sours and sweets in perfect run.
In every bite, a chuckle waits,
The pulp's the truth that resonates.

An orange grin, a grapey grin,
Squeeze the joy from deep within.
These fruity tales will never end,
Let's savor life and just pretend.

Secrets of Sunlit Slices

Beneath bright rays, a tale unfolds,
Citrus slices, secrets bold.
Each bite a giggle, every sip a cheer,
Sunlit corners, laughter near.

Watch the juice drip, a funny sight,
In the kitchen, pure delight.
Sliced and diced, oh what a show,
Zesty laughs just steal the flow.

Wedges glowing, friendship stirs,
Mirthful moments, all preferred.
Secrets shared in vibrant zest,
Laughter rising, feeling blessed.

Lemon, lime, all in the mix,
A fruity dance that truly sticks.
In the sun, our giggles bounce,
Life's sweet nectar, let's pronounce!

The Hidden Essence

In a bowl of colors bright,
Lurking gems, a pure delight.
The essence hides with much flair,
Juicy humor fills the air.

Hidden treasures in each slice,
Tasting laughter, oh so nice.
Squeeze the fun, let's celebrate,
The essence found can't wait, can't wait!

Rinds of laughter, pulp of cheer,
Every segment holds us near.
Crack the shell, discover glee,
Life's sweet juice, come share with me.

From bright rinds to secret sips,
Juicy jests, and playful quips.
In every bite, a chuckle waits,
Let's share this joy that radiates.

The Joys and Pains of Citrus

When life gives you citrus, grab a spoon,
But beware of the juice, it'll make you swoon.
Pithy conversations with friends nearby,
Laughing at faces that wince and cry.

The zest of our laughter fills the air,
As we dodge the seeds with utmost care.
Citrus brightens our plates and moods,
Yet leaves us pondering weird food moods.

A salad of flavors, both sweet and tart,
Each bite a fresh joke, a playful art.
Who knew that a fruit could bring us such glee?
Even if sometimes it tries to flee!

In the end, we embrace each tart twist,
Soured by laughter, can't help but insist.
Citrusy chaos, a comedic delight,
In our fruit-filled world, everything's right!

The Garden's Confession

In the garden, where secrets grow,
A citrus tree waves, putting on a show.
With every bloom, it starts to proclaim,
'Ripe for the picking, but that's just my game!'

The bees come buzzing, a comical sight,
Fumbling their dance, oh, what a fright!
While my neighbor grins, clutching a knife,
Slicing through fruit, oh, the joy of life!

Lemonade dreams and orange delights,
But look out for tangs that lead to fights.
A citrus showdown, who'll take the crown?
A war of flavors, oh, such a clown!

Confessions of joy wrapped in peels,
Every sweet slice, a share of our feels.
Nature's pun, oh, what a thrill,
In this garden of laughter, we've had our fill!

The Sun-Kissed Enigma

On a bright day, under sunshine's gaze,
A round little fruit spins in playful ways.
With a wink and a jiggle, it tempts the hand,
But will it be bitter? Oh, isn't it grand?

Peeling back layers is quite an affair,
Finding surprises hidden with care.
Juicy distractions, oh what a blast!
Each segment a riddle, a puzzle to cast.

Sour faces and giggles, a tricky charade,
As we sip and we slurp these joys we've made.
Is it joy? Is it pain? We laugh and we cry,
Proclaiming our love for citrus up high!

The mystery's sweet, like a riddle divine,
In the sun's embrace, flavors intertwine.
Who knew a fruit could bring such delight?
As we dance in the warmth, everything feels right!

Hidden Depths of Flavor

Beneath the bright skin lies a burst of fun,
With each squirt of juice, our laughter's begun.
A citrus explosion, a zesty surprise,
Revealing the depths, oh how it pries!

Teetering on a balance of tart and sweet,
We pick our favorites, a flavorful feat.
From salads to drinks, the joy we create,
In the funny business of fruit on our plate.

Each bite a giggle, each sip a cheer,
As the flavors play tag, bringing us near.
A fruit that's a prankster, with tricks up its sleeve,
In the clutches of laughter, we always believe!

So here's to the one with the yellowish hue,
For each twist and turn, we give it its due.
In the circle of taste, it dances around,
A comical legend that knows no bound!

The Luminous Heart

In the orchard, bright and bold,
A fruit that wears a crown of gold.
With zest as sharp as a witty jest,
It dances on tongues, a juicy guest.

Its laughter echoes in the breeze,
A citrus tease that aims to please.
Once tasted, friends become a crowd,
For this delight, they sing aloud.

But watch it glow beneath the sun,
It winks and puffs, it loves the fun.
A vibrant heart, it does proclaim,
Life's sweeter with a silly name.

So let us cheer for this delight,
The fruit that sparkles, oh, so bright!
In every slice, a secret cheer,
The laughter whispers, "Eat me, dear!"

Sunlit Secrets

In sunny groves, where laughter grows,
A mystery hides beneath the toes.
With skins so bright, it holds a grin,
This citrus gem where fun begins.

It's not a fable, just a tale,
Of tangy tricks that never pale.
Once you bite, you'll giggle twice,
And dream of how that zest feels nice.

When shared among the merry crowd,
It brings out joy, and laughter loud.
Its sweetness hides a little pulp,
That tickles noses, makes hearts gulp.

So raise a glass to sunny days,
With sips of joy in silly ways.
For every drop that drips and shines,
Is filled with laughter and good times.

Sweet Sorrows of the Grove

A tree stands tall, with arms outspread,
Whispering secrets, a fruity thread.
In every slice, a tale unfolds,
Of sunlit laughter and hearts of gold.

Once picked, it sings a funny song,
Of bittersweet tales that linger long.
With every bite, weird faces bloom,
A fruity giggle dispels the gloom.

Yet in its heart, a pulpy woe,
A hint of pucker it likes to show.
But fear not friends, for laughter's near,
A fruity joke to share and cheer.

So bring a bowl, let's gather round,
With every scoop, let joy abound.
For in the grove, sweet sorrows play,
A citrus love brightens our day.

Beneath the Juicy Surface

A curious fruit, so round and bright,
Challenges taste buds left and right.
With a sly grin, it pulls you in,
Exposing secrets with a spin.

Beneath its skin, a story lies,
Of silly puns and fleeting sighs.
Every wedge hides a zany twist,
A laughing bite, you can't resist.

So slice it up and take a chance,
Let flavors tango, twist, and dance.
In every taste, a chuckle flows,
A winking fruit that always knows.

So grab a spoon, let giggles fly,
For this delight, we can't deny.
With every bite, let joyous mirth,
Reveal the treasures of this earth.

Citrus Ballads of Dawn

In morning light, so bright and bold,
A zesty fruit with tales untold.
With a smile so round and a sun-kissed skin,
It dances and jiggles; let the fun begin!

Its juice, a splash, like lemonade's prank,
A citrus jester in the fruit bank.
When friends gather round for breakfast cheer,
This bouncy ball of joy draws near!

Peeling back layers, oh what a sight,
Squirting juice, oh what a delight!
Each wedge a secret, a giggle, a laugh,
In the fruit salad world, it's the comic half!

So raise your forks, let's toast in glee,
To the citrus wonder, wild and free.
With every bite, let the laughter flow,
A magical start to a zesty show!

The Hidden Harvest

In orange garb, it hides away,
A fruit with perks for a sunny day.
Masked in tang, it waits to surprise,
A burst of flavor, that opens eyes!

With a wink and a nod, it's ready to play,
Small but mighty, it leads the way.
A secret stash in the orchard's fold,
Citrus comedy, ripe and bold!

Its peel unravels, like a magic trick,
A hint of sweetness that dances quick.
Like a clown at a party, it steals the scene,
The life of the grove, so proud and keen!

So gather around, let's share a laugh,
This fruity treasure, it's quite the half!
A jest, a jest, for every bite,
Revealing joy with every bite!

Luminous Citrus Love

Oh, citrus heart, your glow so bright,
With a tangy giggle, you bring delight.
Sliced in half, like love's sweet embrace,
Juices flowing in a funny race!

Your zesty smile, so full of cheer,
Makes breakfast tasty, the best of the year.
Each segment's a story, each bite's a thrill,
A burst of sunshine, a joyous chill!

Oh how you sparkle in the morning light,
Did someone say you're a fruit of delight?
Mutual love, oh, what a hoot,
In the carnival of fruit, you're the star so cute!

So let's lift our forks and share this fun,
Laughing together, all fears overrun.
With citrus love, we joyfully toast,
To this ball of joy, we simply love the most!

Tales from the Orchard Floor

Among the trees where the fruit dreams lay,
Funny tales start to dance and play.
A citrus rogue on the orchard floor,
Spilling secrets, oh, what a score!

Rolling about with a chuckle and grin,
It knows the joy that lies within.
Each juicy segment a playful riddle,
Giving giggles like a quirky fiddle!

With every bite there's a tale to share,
A twist, a turn, a citrus affair.
Such grand adventures, with laughter galore,
In the orchard's embrace, we crave for more!

So join the fun, don't sit alone,
In this citrus kingdom, you've found a home.
Where laughter echoes and sweet tales soar,
The orchard's secrets, you'll adore!

The Untold Flavor

In a bowl, it sits so round,
Whispers of sweetness abound.
It teases taste buds, oh so bright,
A juicy jest, a fruity delight.

With each bite, a giggle slips,
Tart surprises, zesty drips.
Sour friends and sweet ones play,
In this citrus charade, come what may.

Beneath the Silken Skin

Underneath that vibrant coat,
Lies a tale, oh what a quote!
A chuckle lurks, a tangy cheer,
Each section sings, 'I'm happy here!'

Peeling back its bright façade,
A comedy of flavors, oh so odd.
With laughter packed in every slice,
Each taste a twist, oh isn't that nice?

Layers of Citrus Mystique

A riddle wrapped in citrus zest,
What's sour can often be the best.
Unpeel the layers, start to explore,
Each segment opens a whimsical door.

With a wink, the juice spills wide,
On taste buds, it knows it can glide.
A playful jest in every bite,
This sun-kissed fruit feels just right.

Taradiddle in Citrus

A fib in every juicy slice,
Promises sweet, but rolls the dice.
A tale of tang that twists and turns,
In every peel, a laugh that burns.

With every zest, a stinging jest,
A citric giggle, oh what a quest!
So take a bite, let humor spill,
In this fruity frolic, taste the thrill.

Twilight Citrus Secrets

In twilight's glow, a fruit does smile,
Its zesty laugh a playful style.
Beneath the skin, a joke it keeps,
A punchline ripe, as daylight sleeps.

The moonlit dance of citrus cheer,
With every slice, we shed our fear.
Juice drips down like giggles bright,
As we uncork a fun-filled night.

Twisted peels in laughter twine,
Like secret friends in citrus brine.
With every taste, a quirky jest,
A punch of sweetness, we are blessed.

So laugh aloud, don't hold it in,
With every bite, let humor spin.
In fruity bliss, our worries cease,
These twilight tales, a fruity feast.

The Bitter and the Sweet

A wedge of life, both sharp and round,
It balances on laughter's ground.
The tart and sweet in playful chat,
A fruity duel, imagine that!

With every crunch, a truth revealed,
That laughter's juice cannot be sealed.
A hint of grim, a burst of glee,
In every bite, a mystery.

So take a slice, embrace the blend,
A citrus turn, around the bend.
In this sweet world, a joke does seep,
For every laugh, there's joy to keep.

From bitter roots, the laughter grows,
Citrus secrets only humor knows.
A playful twist, a silly treat,
In every bite, the bittersweet.

Slices of Solitude

In solitude, a fruit so bright,
A private laugh, a tasty bite.
Each slice reveals a cheeky grin,
A solo party tucked within.

The world outside may seem quite drear,
But citrus laughs can draw us near.
In every segment lies a jest,
A funny truth, our hearts caressed.

So peel away the silent night,
Let laughter burst in citrus light.
From one small fruit, pure joy can grow,
In solitude, we steal the show.

So savor days of peace and zest,
Where humor finds its perfect nest.
Each segment sliced, a giggle shared,
In quiet moments, we are bared.

Citrus Canopy Whispers

Beneath the leaves, a riddle hums,
In citrus groves, the humor comes.
With every rustle, secrets spill,
As laughter dances, we stand still.

The canopy a stage for glee,
Fruitful whispers, wild and free.
Zesty puns like raindrops fall,
In this lush world, we hear the call.

With tangy zest, the branches sway,
Tickling thoughts, through skies of gray.
In fruity realms, our giggles sprout,
And citrus joy is roundabout.

So join the whispers, take a chance,
In citrus shadows, let's all dance.
With every leaf, the laughter grows,
In this wild fruit potpourri, it shows.

A Tangy Riddle

In a garden bright and sunny,

A fruit with zest, oh so funny.
An orange's cousin, round and bold,
A twist of taste, a story told.

Peel its skin, a burst of cheer,
Oh, dear friend, that flavor's near.
Puckered lips and giggles shared,
With every bite, we feel ensnared.

What's more fun, it's not a bear,
It's citrus joy beyond compare!
A juicy jest in every slice,
Life's zingy prank, oh so nice!

In every wedge, a riddle spun,
A tangy tale, a juicing run.
We'll laugh and munch, no one will know,
The citrus nerds put on a show!

The Aroma That Lingers

A scent that dances in the air,

With tangy notes beyond compare.
As I slice through, the zest awakes,
A fragrant laugh, a tease, and quakes.

The juice erupts, it splatters wide,
A citrus shower, oh, what a ride!
Smiles burst like bubbles in the sun,
With every squirt, more giggles run.

In the kitchen chaos, fun prevails,
As laughter echoes over citrus tales.
What strange delight, such joy we find,
In slicing secrets, oh so blind!

With every whiff, we start to play,
A zesty game that brightens the day.
So hold your nose and take a chance,
Let's citrus twist and do a dance!

Secrets of the Citrus Grove

Under leaves where sunbeams play,

A mystery hides in bright display.
A globe of sunshine, round and bright,
Chasing laughs from dawn till night.

What hides inside? A fragrant joke,
Sour and sweet, a fruit that spoke.
Among the branches, giggles bloom,
In every nook, it fills the room.

The trees all chuckle, roots entwined,
In citrus laughter, we're combined.
Every fruit with tales to tell,
In juicy whispers, all is swell.

So gather round and come unwind,
In zesty laughter, joy will find.
Each bite reveals a tasty scheme,
In this grove, we laugh and dream!

Bittersweet Confessions

I took a bite, oh, what a twist,

A tart rebuke I can't resist.
With puckered face and tearful glee,
The fruit of secrets shines for me.

A sour kiss, a sweet delight,
This fruit knows how to spark a fight.
With every taste, a silly sigh,
As citrus giggles float on by.

Did you hear that? A slice unveils,
A funny tale the tongue regales.
In every spoonful, quirks unfold,
A bittersweet plot, brave and bold.

So let us share this laugh-filled treat,
With every bite, bittersweet feat.
For the truths we find, wrapped in zest,
Citrus confessions, we are blessed!

Juicy Mysteries Unveiled

In the orchard, shadows creep,
Citrus whispers, secrets keep.
Droplets dance on zesty skin,
What lies beneath, let's begin!

A slice revealed, a twist, a turn,
Does the orange have a plan to spurn?
With every squirt, a giggle too,
A fruity riddle, what will it do?

Beneath the peel, a world so bright,
Teasing taste buds, pure delight.
Spreading smiles, one juicy jest,
A tangy game, come join the fest!

So gather 'round, let laughter ring,
As quirks of fruit weave tales to sing.
In every bite, surprise awaits,
Unravel now, this mystery of states!

Orange Hues and Hidden Clues

In sunny fields where citrus thrives,
Laughter bubbles, joy arrives.
A dash of zest, a flick of rind,
What crazy tales are intertwined?

Behind the frolic, juicy smiles,
Tangled flavors in playful piles.
Each section hides a pun so sly,
Peel it back, give it a try!

The pith could share a tale or two,
Of squirrels dressed in orange hue.
Mischief lingers where fruit does roll,
In every slice, a jester's soul.

So grab a wedge, let giggles bloom,
In this orchard full of room.
Where color clashes, and tastes collide,
In citrus dreams, our truths abide!

Fragrant Truths

In fragrant groves, mysteries blend,
Each juicy globe, a playful friend.
Tangy notes in the summer breeze,
What fragrant truths hide 'neath the trees?

With every peel, a chuckle spills,
A citrus circus that time fulfills.
Squirrels giggle, as they partake,
A riddle wrapped in zestful flake.

A citrus twist upon my plate,
Sunshine antics never wait.
Sour patches and sweet delights,
Oh, what joy, in fruity fights!

So munch away, embrace the cheer,
In every bite, a story near.
A banquet rich in flavors bold,
Fragrant truths best left untold!

A Peel of Intrigue

Beneath the skin, a tale unfolds,
Of sneaky smiles and citrus golds.
With every twist, a laugh erupts,
In this orchard, joy interrupts.

Vibrant shades of sunset skies,
Fruits conceal their fun disguise.
What tricks await upon the branch?
Can you solve this zesty dance?

Now squeeze it tight, release the fun,
The citrus jest has just begun.
Pulp and pulp make laughter rise,
Unravel truths beneath those eyes.

So join the feast, and take a bite,
Where every fruit is pure delight.
In this riddle, with humor shared,
A peel of intrigue, always dared!

The Silken Citrus Embrace

In a world of tangy bites,
Fruit takes on curious feats.
Peel away the bitter skins,
Joy and silliness repeats.

Juicy arcs, a yellow-red glow,
Pulp dancing in midday sun.
Laughs burst with every squeeze,
Taste buds now have lots of fun.

Sweet laughter fills the air,
As friends gather 'round to share.
Citrus smiles in every slice,
Puns and giggles, oh so nice!

A zestful twist, a fruity spin,
Serious faces can't win.
In this tangy, playful game,
We're all slightly insane!

Layers of Sunlight and Shade

Peeling back the sunlit zest,
What a crazy, funny quest!
In each layer, laughs reside,
Bright and cheeky, can't confide.

Round and round, the jokes do roll,
With every sip, we lose control.
Citrus segments steal the show,
Playful tongues, they twist and flow.

Underneath the bright facade,
A squirt of joy, if you've had.
Sunshine drinks in glasses tall,
Who said fruit can't break the stall?

In the shade of sweet delight,
Jokes abound, it feels so right.
Nature's way to make us smile,
Stay a while, it's worth your while!

The Citrus Epiphany

A burst of flavor in my hand,
Sudden giggles, life is grand.
With each slice, revelation,
Fruit and fun, pure celebration.

Lemon twists and orange cheer,
A citrus smile brings you near.
Beneath the peel, a world unseen,
A fruity laugh machine so keen.

Who knew such joy could be found,
In a fruit with tang abound?
Every pucker faces fate,
Turns our frowns to something great!

Life's a drink that's fresh and bright,
Sparkling laughter, pure delight.
So come and taste this zestful glee,
Unlocking joy, just like a key!

A Symphony of Citrus Dreams

In orchards filled with sunny tunes,
Citrus dances, and laughter swoons.
Every bite a playful quip,
A citrus dream, let's take a trip!

Moments bright, with zest accrued,
Squeezed together, we are renewed.
Bitter sweet, a mix so fine,
In this symphony, let's all dine.

With every drop, a story told,
Of silly faces, brave and bold.
Lively hues, from sun to shade,
In this fruity parade, we're made!

A concert of flavors in our hands,
Harmony where fun expands.
Explore the thrill within each bite,
Citrus dreams that spark delight!

The Lush Citrus Tapestry

In gardens bright with citrus cheer,
Lemons grinning ear to ear.
An orange giggled, pink in hue,
Saying, "Come on, join the crew!"

A peel slipped off, a bouncy dance,
Citrus fruits in sunshine prance.
Pineapple shared a fruit punch joke,
Grapes rolled by, all in a cloak.

Limes played tag with juicy flair,
While cherries giggled in despair.
The oranges formed a jolly band,
Creating juice, oh so grand!

With every squirt, each rind's delight,
The zest of life shines ever bright.
No secrets here, just tasty mirth,
In this citrus-colored Earth!

In the Wake of Zest

A fruit parade upon a plate,
Where flavors mingle, it's first-rate.
The yellow ones begin to jest,
While sweet surprises take their rest.

With every slice, a witty tale,
Of lemon pranks that never fail.
Grapefruits giggle, "We're the best!"
While apples wink, "We love the zest!"

Cantaloupes chase the juicy bliss,
As melons plot their summer kiss.
They dance around the bubbling brew,
A funny fest, with every hue.

In this circus of juicy cheer,
The fruit folks gather, spreading cheer.
Not a secret, just laughs galore,
As zestful joy's hard to ignore!

A Citrus Sonnet

Oh, citrus world, a zesty whim,
Where flavors dance on every brim.
A sparkling laugh, a tangy grin,
Where fruity follies all begin.

The grapefruits flaunt their funny zest,
While cantaloupes ponder their best.
Oranges giggle, sharing a tale,
While juicy limes set forth a trail.

In fruitland's arms, no secrets hide,
Just laughter bubbling, side by side.
A whirlwind twist of every taste,
As sweetness reigns, no time to waste!

So here we gather, all in fun,
In this tart kingdom, under the sun.
Each bite a giggle, sharp or sweet,
In this vibrant, zestful seat!

Unraveled Flavor Fables

Once upon a time, they say,
Fruits told stories in a zesty way.
Lemon-lore met orange rhyme,
Crafting tales, one juicy time.

The tangy twist of grapefruit bold,
Shared laughter that never gets old.
Watermelon cracked a silly grin,
As peach pie jokes began to spin.

Pineapple danced with coconut cheer,
While cherries hummed a fruity seer.
In this land where flavors tease,
The zest erupted with playful ease.

So grab a slice, join the brigade,
In this juicy world where secrets fade.
No mysteries, just comedic bliss,
In the fruit fable, a citrus kiss!

The Aroma of Truth

In the kitchen, a scent so bright,
Takes me back to a citrus delight.
Juicy drops, a tart little tease,
Revealing secrets among the leaves.

With every slice, a splash of juice,
The laughter builds, a funny ruse.
Peeling back layers, oh what a treat,
Surprises lurk in every sweet beat.

Sour faces turn giggles in time,
As citrus tang adds to the rhyme.
A fruit that plays hide and seek,
Turns every frown into a cheeky peek.

So let's toast to the zest in life,
With every bite, we banish strife.
A playful twist on what we ate,
Oh, how these fruits just love to bait!

A Symphony of Citrus

Squeeze me softly, a zesty sound,
In a symphony, joy is found.
A burst of flavor that makes you grin,
Sharing laughs, let the fun begin.

Notes of sour play a charming tune,
Dancing fruits under a full moon.
The tangy harmony fills the air,
With every bite, there's laughter to spare.

Mixed with sugar or cooked in pie,
Sweet and sour, oh me, oh my!
A citrus orchestra, we all unite,
Creating giggles, oh what delight!

So gather your friends, let's make a mess,
With citrus wonders, we're truly blessed.
A tasty concert we won't forget,
Each bite a joy, each laugh a bet!

Citrus Tales Untold

In a grove, a tale unfolds,
Of juicy cheeks and secrets bold.
A citrus twist, a giggly cheer,
Whispered tales for all to hear.

With every wedge, a story spills,
Of silly smiles and playful thrills.
Peeling back layers, laughter grows,
Citrus humor, everybody knows.

A slice of life, no need for care,
Just fruity fun, it's everywhere!
From brunch to snacks, let laughter reign,
In every drop, a sweet refrain.

So hold that fruit with a wink and grin,
Join the fun, let the jokes begin.
Citrus tales, let's share them all,
With every bite, we laugh and sprawl!

Flesh and Fable

In the heart, a story lies,
Swirling sweetness, a fun surprise.
Flesh so juicy, a tale's embrace,
Bringing smiles to every face.

Fables told in every bite,
Citrus magic, pure delight.
With a squirt, a laugh erupts,
While silly puns get all mixed up.

Fiction pairs with rind so bright,
A playful twist in every bite.
Laughter echoes, the room ignites,
As fruit delivers quirky sights.

So slice away with glee and zest,
Each fruity tale is truly blessed.
Flesh and fable in perfect tune,
We'll laugh and dance beneath the moon!

Citrus Labyrinth of Flavor

In a maze of zest, I roam so free,
Pungent pathways lead to a briny spree.
Oranges giggle, lemons dance around,
While lime plays tricks, never to be found.

A tangerine whispers, 'Don't eat me raw!'
Waves of citrus laughter, what a raucous draw!
Underneath the rinds, flavors collide,
In this juicy world, there's nowhere to hide.

With every bite, a squirty surprise,
Juicy friendships bloom beneath the skies.
Grapefruits gossip, sharing their tales,
In this citrus circus, fun never fails.

So I spin through the tangy, sweet, and sour,
In this labyrinth of zest, I'm ruled by power.
With each vibrant segment, I'm hooting in cheer,
Navigating flavors, with no cause for fear.

The Unseen Citrus Universe

In a cosmos of citrus, stars shine so bright,
Orange comets zoom, adding sweet delight.
Lemon moons twinkle, sour beams they cast,
While grapefruits laugh, oh, what a bold blast!

Galaxies spin in a zesty embrace,
With tangy tales woven in perfect grace.
A universe hidden, yet bursting with cheer,
Each slice reveals wonders, exquisite and clear.

Pluto's a lime, chilling out in the shade,
And Mars is a mango, but I'm not afraid!
Through the citrus skyways, I float with glee,
In this fruity galaxy, just you and me.

Asteroids of flavor crash into my plate,
As I navigate through this delicious fate.
Unseen delights lead me on, what a ride!
In this universe, I'm eager and filled with pride.

Confessions of a Tangy Heart

Oh, my heart's a fruit, so tangy and spry,
With a zest for life, I simply can't lie.
I flirt with a citrus, all bright and bold,
In sweet little secrets, our stories unfold.

Lemon and lime, they tease me each night,
While oranges cheer me, oh what a sight!
I'd spill my heart juice, if given the chance,
In this fruity affair, I might just dance.

Confessions are splashed with colors so bright,
As I juggle these fruits, what a silly flight!
With every bite taken, my secrets flow free,
In the purest of joy, I find my decree.

So here's to the tangy, a love that's arrived,
In a citrusy world, I've happily thrived.
With patterns of flavor, my heart beats with glee,
In this juicy saga, I'm perfectly me.

The Citrus Paradox

Oh, what a fruit, so sweet yet so tart,
A juicy riddle that tickles the heart.
To bite or to sip, what will it be?
A paradox wrapped in a zesty decree!

A peel that entices, a juice that can stun,
Within every citrus, lies laughter and fun.
Mix up a cocktail, or nibble a slice,
The sweet-sour dance is oh-so-nice!

Behold the dilemma of flavor divine,
Do I want a twist, or perhaps just some brine?
In this citrus kingdom where giggles abound,
I'm caught in a whirlwind of flavor unbound.

So toss me a fruit salad, let's mix and swirl,
In this citrus paradox, let joy unfurl.
With zest-filled adventures that never will cease,
I find my delight in this tangy peace.

The Soul Beneath the Zest

In morning light, a peel so bright,
It guards a treasure, oh what a sight!
A flavor twist, like a cheeky jest,
A burst of joy, in every zest.

It giggles loud, when sliced in half,
With juice that dances, oh what a laugh!
A pucker here, a grin up high,
A citrus prank, oh my! Oh my!

Behind the tang, a tale unfolds,
Of sunny days and laughter bold.
It whispers secrets through every slice,
A comedy act, oh so precise!

So take a bite, and let it sing,
A playful note, a zesty spring.
In every wedge, a giggle grows,
Beneath the skin, the fun just flows!

Aromatic Enigmas

In a bowl of fruit, a puzzling orb,
With mystery wrapped, it can absorb.
A fragrant riddle, in zest it hides,
Its wittiest jokes, the taste confides.

Peel back the layers, take a sniff,
A citrus charm, is this a myth?
Sweet and sour, a playful mix,
In every slice, a laugh that clicks!

It rolls on the counter, with a grin,
Challenging all, 'Come, take me in!'
With every section, a new surprise,
A fragrant show, that tickles your eyes.

So grab a spoon, and scoop it right,
This little orb is pure delight.
Its aromatic laugh will lift your mood,
In every bite, just tasty food!

Soursweet Chronicles

Once upon a time, in fruitland bright,
Lived a cheeky orb, full of light.
With a sassy grin, it told a tale,
Of soursweet joy that would never pale.

Its citrus crown, a wobbly hat,
Bouncing along, where's the cat?
A zingy dance, with every peel,
It spins the plot, oh what a reel!

In juicy drops, the stories flow,
Of sunny skies and rainbows' glow.
Each segment holds a quirky jest,
A flavorsome journey, that beats the rest.

So join the fun, grab a fork,
Dive into flavor, that will not cork.
With laughter shared, in every bite,
This soursweet journey is pure delight!

Liquid Sunrise

The morning sun spills juice so bright,
A golden ocean, pure delight!
In a glass it giggles, waves all around,
A merry splash, with a happy sound.

Citrus waves crash on tastebud shores,
With every sip, a joy that soars.
A zesty dance, a playful swirl,
It tickles your tongue, oh what a twirl!

So lift your glass, to sunny cheer,
The liquid laugh, that draws us near.
Floating fruit in the morning haze,
Brings laughter out in delightful ways.

Embrace the dawn, in citrus style,
With every sip, let's share a smile!
For in this cup, a day begins,
With liquid sunshine and tasty spins!

www.ingramcontent.com/pod-product-compliance
Lightning Source LLC
Chambersburg PA
CBHW070007300426
43661CB00141B/359